An Observer's Ledger:

A Poetry Collection

Anil Kumar Vinayak

BookLeaf
Publishing

Presentation by *BookLeaf Publishing*

Web: www.bookleafpub.com

E-mail: info@bookleafpub.com

ISBN: 9789360943318

First edition 2024

*Dedicated to those I've had the fortune to cross paths with
&
to those who lent a moment to glance at my scribbles ...*

Preface

To wander is not a vice, but it sure is a double-edged sword that has been blunted enough to deny them reprieve. I penned my first poem out of boredom and the rest I attribute to expression. However, the harsher days or those left over for thought or other pensive pastimes needed a vent and a pen and paper were the only elements that could contain the volcanic eruptions of a rambling mind. While my first poetry collection examined the punctuations in a busy world, this one holds the compilation of a wandering mind and body. Every poem here was inspired by the "every day" which typically is more beautiful in retrospect than in the present. I can't offer much but I hope the little that is provided makes way for greater introspection.

Anil Kumar Vinayak (Vin)

Contents

Due South

Due south he goes on the northbound train,
A journey destined to end in vain.
The rocking lullaby rolled thoughts to dreams,
Lost in them was the listless pilgrim.

Raindrops thudded on the speckled glass,
Jolting him awake, dreams dashed alas!
The remnants of his slumber rattled by thunder,
Sobriety ripped his peace asunder.

Burdened by 'what was' & bruised by 'what could
be',
Due south he hurtled on the beaten path.

-Vin

Carnival Delights

Without a care, happy and bare
We traversed a carnival fair;
Merry-Go-Rounds and Tilt-A-Whirls,
On we marched as the flags unfurled.

The days dimmed and the joy alighted;
Two decades and a few,
Never again the heart so flew;
The Ferris Wheel now, seems sad and blue.

The Tilts till swirl & the Rounds are merry,
But the lil' man's not invited on that ferry.
He picked up his bread and expired cheese,
The carnival delights were a cruel tease.

Fortune, fate and destiny,
They locked him outta that fair.

-Vin

Ides of Spring

Bid adieu to the badlands,
decked in snow & devoid of life
Filled with nothing but the vagaries of strife;
Here ends the chill of the northern winds.

Greet the morning sun with a tinge of fun,
A bluejay's song to beat the Monday blues.
Brimming with the promise of a better
tomorrow,
The glory of Springtide has just begun.

A world reborn in the image of hope,
How long before we bid you adieu?

-Vin

Left Behind

In the wake of a lullaby
Lost was the thought;
The scent of her seared into his heart.
When all farewells bid a final goodbye,
Nothing but a shadow was left behind.

People that left, places left behind,
Memories remained while moments persisted;
The image of her failed the wretched blind.
So ends today with no promise of tomorrow,
Choose thy battles, the ones to lose -
She's just a daydream to douse the flame?

- Vin

How long, Lily?

Fall floods the horizon,
A threatening chill chuckles beyond;
Nurtured from nothing
to the luscious lushness of plenty,
Her lilac petals pale
before the perils to come.

Mist, murking and mirthless,
plucks at the sulking strings
to punish the witnessing night as
Lily burns to an unbeloved brown...

Silence tolls at the scornful sirens,
Time had torn her flowery soul.

-Vin

Back alleys

Born in embrace, brought to disgrace;
Back alleys grieved for the bachelor's passing.
To venture beyond the vulture's vice,
To see the dregs of dulled devices.

Hear and fear the alleys out back,
A barren land bereft of barricades.
Bellow the names holed beyond the dark;
Villains of virtue, lay down your mark.

Listen and learn from the leaden lads,
For the bad and the bred have played their cards.

-Vin

Wounded Valley

Far away in the farthest corners,
Spruce and snow seduces the eyes.
Herbs once deemed the devil's ruse,
Here it flows, hot and profuse.
The cold that chills, the frost that kills,
The faraway land promised fairer shores.

Neither hallowed, never holy;
Could this be the one true folly?
The valley beckons with indifferent wonder,
For her beauty once, was bled asunder.

-Vin

The House

Solitary in a game of solitaire,
Led afar by the buzz of winter fair,
nestled the house in need of a spouse.

Flanked by concrete behemoths,
Furloughed by suited scythes,
The house crumbled as the keeper fumbled.

The tone of morn awakens monotony's drone,
The House on the prairie stifled a yawn.

What was to become of what was left?
The house was to weep for faith bereft.

Snow and sun, arm in arm;
Penury does do some harm.

-Vin

Festive

Magic in the air & meringue snowmen for
company,
The festive red holds tight for merry multifold.
Come 'n rejoice the break from broken work,
'Tis the season to welcome joy aboard.

Let bygones be bygones, let grudges turn to
fudge;
The air be jolly so don't drown in past folly.
Make amends & make merry,
'Tis the season to board the friendly ferry.

Festive be the day and so the chilly nights,
May the spirits soar with delightful might!!!

-Vin

Dying Daffodils

Wordsworth was smitten by golden daffodils,
All I've left now are concrete and chills.
The sunflowers that once longed for Apollo's
gold,
Now can no longer hold his gaze,
For they be withered by whims of old.
The stench of garbage subjugates the rose,
The blackish air smothers her red.

What have we done!? What can we do?
All that is left is rubble and rubbish.
To err maybe human but to destroy is definitely
man.

The wheels have turned and life might spew,
But the future's got no rainbows;
Just silicon and wires.

So let us wallow in our impending doom,
For the deserts have begun to snow.

-Vin

Luna

A scarab amulet adorned her neck,
Beautiful then but buried now between the
wrecks.
There was a tingling when he first saw her,
A sentient night honored the witness's chore.
Fair maiden amongst the unfair black,
Fighting for freedom from fallacy ridden flak.
He gazed with the gloom of inevitable doom,
For he has fallen for the tomb.

Through watery eyes he gazed at the heavens,
"I've always loved you."

Tonight she shines bright,
Waiting for another to hold her gaze.

-Vin

Cometh the Spring

And so comes the end of Winter,
No cold to brave 'nd chills to tear asunder.
Cometh the morn 'nd the sweet smell of spring,
The scent of fresh blooms bursting into song.

Heal thy wounds and heed thy thoughts,
Leave your sorrows with the snow of wintertide.

Beauty basking under the glorious sun,
Let new life bring gaiety and fun.

-Vin

Reason to Stay

Far from the sea and beyond the hills,
On the prairies due north where the wind is
shrill;
A city sleeps in the midst of a blizzard.
Far and forlorn but filled with life,
The town does teem with harmonious strife.

So came a soul who's passing by,
Not held to the city by kith nor kin.
The days were odd and the nights were hard,
So were the adventures of the vagabond bard.

Then in folly came a thought so unholy,
He pondered a penance on these perilous
prairies;
The Wanderer willed for wood to call home.

Far from the sea and beyond the hills,
A Reason to Stay quelled all reasoning...

-Vin

A Moment More

On the brink of winter at the border of fall,
A silent hum had silenced the song.
It's time for goodbyes
But you've said'em twice too soon.
Am headed south on the northbound train,
Need to shake the pain of your disdain.

Why did we become you and me,
When tomorrow told us we'll be free.
Why did we ever cross paths,
When I had to bear the cross of your wrath.
A bit of you is stuck in all of me,
Can never heal the scars of your touch.

Will 'morrow bring a dew of hope
Or will sorrow knot the rough hemp rope?
A treasure I'll trade for a moment more...

A moment more in your embrace
A moment more to kiss you anew.

-Vin

The Lone Traveller

Listless but full of lust,
The bed ridden Traveller was the epitome of
pathetic.
Dry lips murmuring in a feverish stupor,
Riddled with visions he dare not utter.
It was time to make the ultimate journey.
However, there was one regret,
Just the one.
In all his travels, be it business or pleasure,
He was on a secret quest for treasure,
Not gold or the wisdom of old
But that is dear to a man's heart,
Or so he was told....

Somewhere untouched by civilization,
Lays the corpse of The Lone Traveller.

-Vin

Beauty Unlike

As far as the eye can see,
As beautiful as the day can be;
A patch of green and patterns of dew,
Memories covered up in that tender hue.

Beauty, my dear, can be found in the most
unlikely of places,
if only one does dare to look.

-Vin

Familiar

He grumbled along till he mumbled to sleep,
A tinge of irony as he called earth's own heaven
home.
Then that day dawned and packed bags sent him
afar;
Not a life to covet but one to coerce survival.
And in that darkness he saw a flame,
novel but strangely familiar;
Then it hit, the damned realization:
It was a flame from the beauty he once
bemoaned,
A life before packed bags,
In a paradise he refused to explore.

-Vin

Red & Gold

The river mirrored the red and gold,
beside the abode of the glittery God;
Another day of damned futility,
awaiting the divine deluge of tomorrow.
The paranoia shattered by the colors abound,
aided by birds bound for the horizon.

And just like that,
The world froze in red and gold;
Dear Lord! It's time to head home.

-Vin

The Iron Gate

Along what lay beyond,
usurped by an unknown terror,
The Boy stared at the ferrous gates
with a frown followed by a frantic thumping.
Time had robbed the behemoth of its strength;
The hinges that once opened like a quiet stream,
now huffed and puffed with a rusty scream.
The Boy looked on with curiosity
vanquishing his dread
wondering what lay beyond the iron giant.

-Vin

Blind Faith

Live with a longing,
lie without a conscience;
Rhetoric trumps reality and reason be a runny
ruse.
To trust the face at face value,
with no concern for true value; "Believe me
Good Sirs and Gentle Ladies, for your trust is
safe with me!"

Faith that is forty fathoms deep
and fetid with fatuous fallacies,
be the gateway to your furrowed demise.
Beware of the better folk;
Be wary of the fickle charlatans;
Most importantly,
ponder before you lease your heart,
for those tenuous tenants could get a tad tedious
to evict.

Trust has no Braille;
Thus the blind is left illiterate in Faith.

-Vin

A Night of Pleasure

A whiff of red roses and a world of pleasure,
his hands moved down her curves in search of
treasure.
Gently caressing her glistening back
with time tied to its tenuous tracks;
The melodies of love consumed by the rhythm of
lust,
tears of pleasure dripping down with every
thrust.

A moment of tranquility;
A scream of blissful ecstasy.
The night was complete and the neighbors slept
on.

Flushed with furious fervor
and panting with pernicious power;
A rustling of the leaves and the night was choked
in silence.

-Vin

Concrete Jungle

Aroma of spices and clinking of glasses
spaced with idle chatter and business mergers.
A breeze arose from the concrete jungle,
chilly and soft with the smell of the sea.
It was time for dessert and formal adieus;
a match was made in corporate heaven
and the beasts returned to their concrete caves.

-Vin

A Box of Chocolates

A medley of many but symphony of none;
Musing over the sweeter things and mindless of
the sour.
Forgive the soul who has grown dour,
For it be a pain to be plain and pathetic.

Let it rest amidst a box of chocolates
and savor the silly stories,
For a mama once said,
"You never know what you're gonna get".

-Vin

Red

Untamed by the blood moon,
Her hair bellowed in the hands of salty winds.
A little too crimson but none too deep,
the gash on her arm let the simple blood weep.
In a minute or two her world will turn black,
but for now her scarlet company held her intact.

In time she became a memory;
A bunch of red roses beginning to wither.

-Vin

The Sketch

The darker hues brought her to life,
Charred remains when indecision was rife.
She was none he knew,
Another pencil stroke on white canvas.
Soon but soon the eyes would stare,
Far beyond than he'd care.
He thought of glimmer and glitter:
Anything to bring her closer to the world of men.
But then something formed in the corner of her
eye,
Her soul effused the bitter truth.
She was shackled to the flat dimensions,
For beyond the paper she was just a thought:
An artist's stroke of genius.

-Vin

The Wrecks

She took'em all, big and small;
Her bosom adorned with floating corpses.
The men of the sea succumbed to her wills,
Whilst the tempest raged and their vessel caved.

The carrion was her's to keep,
A trophy for her winged children;
10 moons later the wood washed ashore,
A kingdom devoid of its beloved subjects.
100 moons later the wood turned to dust,
The screams muffled by rusty nails.

1000 moons later the wood would be gone,
And along with it, the memories of screaming
corpses.

-Vin

Barren

Rocks and dust and barren hills,
the mountain goats bleat while the eagle circles;
A stream of water would be no less a miracle.
Through thick and thin and thoughtless trudges
emerges the mirage of an oasis beyond.
Let them boil in the heat of golden toil,
and the last plant withers for want of fertile soil.
To be lost in a land seldom traversed:
he shouldn't have chosen the road less traveled.

-Vin

Bottled Poetry

In times of duress and dubious joy,
The elixir of gods tingle thy tongues.
To please it does and make pleasant it dances,
The courage of commoners and kiln of inept
craftsmen.
It slips down like a comforting caress,
Blurring the moment between triumph and
tribulation.
It be misunderstood to be the devil bottled in,
Be not fooled for the genie awaits
And the wishes go beyond the triple.
So let it flow through you,
Dear soul in dire need;
For what awaits you is poetry in a bottle.

-Vin

Lotus

Bloom and wither like all things living,
Motif of survival and marvelous at the close;
Neck deep but not drowning yet,
The still waters are never weary.
Retribution be branded on perceived slights,
Reason be sold to undue scruples.
Gentle, be gentle and let it be;
Easy on the eye,
Bounded by the easel of grief.

-Vin

Raspberry Relish

Warm day and a broken breeze,
I yearned for some shade and a bottle of Freez.
Took succour under the white canopy
in the café of yoghurts tingling with chattering
melodies.

An order of their finest was made,
And i was bestowed the honor of adorning it.
Took a long hard look at the sugary concoctions
laid out for me
with their fruity peers frantic in color.
Berries and syrups and M&Ms and caramel;
My my, the dilemma of choice!!

Then the red of somewhat infamous fame
frowned at me,
"My crimson will cradle your milky mixture",
they yawped.
I acquiesced and acquired my cup of crimson
delights,
A flavor to savor and a fragrance to not forget.

-Vin

Lady Earth's Fury

Fan the flames of forgotten embers,
The fury of the fallen will cease to falter.
The blunders that burden those burnt souls,
Kindled in the kilns by callous palms.
In search of Retribution not wanting of glory,
Beware, dear reader, this not a happy story.
hakes,
Trading drudgery for full stomachs.

Yet it lingered, the abominable dream.
An urge to let the wind in my hair,
To let our hips sway to the rhythm of blue;
To hold you closer till it was all black.

But she was there, she always was.
Weaving into his poems,
Perched atop the celestial darkness.
It was a full moon tonight.

-Vin

Dark Clouds

A sense of foreboding and the drizzle of
humorless rain,
A pinch of irony and the subtlety of pain;
Drawn by indifference the green and blue,
Brows clouded by greying frowns.
Wind in his hair and tears in his eyes,
It was all goodbyes to the gentle heaven's cries.
Behold the beauty of bountiful bereavement;
The smell of wet soil wafts content.

-Vin

River

Gentle waves caressed the shore,
A new day poised to come ashore.
The bench was empty and the breeze was
company,
That was normal and he sought no epiphany.
Trounced by time and tasting metal,
Little was left of his joyful mettle.

The river's lullaby was crooning him to sleep,
The water kissing his shoes;
He longed to follow her where the wind took her,
'Maybe tomorrow', the muttered consolation.

-Vin

Helpless

That which haunts the merry minds of men
In sobriety and those of sound mind,
Bled dry by routine and roulettes,
Decked on the crust of the dessert of decadence.

Hand outstretched from that numbing inferno,
Longing to escape the horrors of hope.
In tomorrow's world of sorrow and cancerous
marrows,
These helpless hands will flail in the sweltering
air.

-Vin

A Father's Son

The title conferred when life is made,
Hopes and dreams kindled anew.
A tale so old that cliché evolves to routine.
A man be made and a man be bred,
Like his father and his father before him.

To better him and be better at,
A hefty legacy to live upto.
In all of life, failure is one:
Rob the Father's pride
by ineptitude and folly.

-Vin

Mermaid

The curls on her hair danced with the waves,
Prisoner of the Seas, what do you crave?
Amidst the blue vastness you call home,
I be just an interloper destined to roam.

Until the night my buoyant home wrecks,
I be safe in a drudgery worth my name.
Alas! I fear we may never meet.
Lady of the sea,
Be so ever gentle while you grant me eternal
peace.

-Vin

Rugged River

37

On the river that flows forth with vengeance and
venom,
He had built his dam from damned dividends.
By force he fans the famished embers,
To remember the wounds that the river wrought.
He had tamed the turbulent waters,
But the poison that persists can never be purged.
So beware warrior of the valleys of valor,
The river be stopped but the rigours not lost.

-Vin

Mediocre

There was beauty in mediocrity,
But never was there glory.
Tiptoe around half-cooked portions,
No prize to show but daily rations.
Prosper to please,
Ironed resumés with no crease.

Time has run out,
Tenderness long gone,
No tales to tell,
No texts to send.

His last breath was usual, average, mediocre.

-Vin

Sobriety Awaits

To rise and fall before the sun and after the
moon,
Reality is no reprieve and romanticism is
reserved for the rich and ripe.
Escape to the deepest depths of the poetic mind,
A gentle push and the road less traveled seems
all the less sinister.
It's a smoky haze with a dreary pace,
All but save the lull in libertarian values.
Leave now with the head abuzz,
For sobriety awaits every Monday morning.

-Vin

The Port

As she gazed upon the port of blue,
Ships docked and sailors aboard,
Fishermen haggling and sea gulls cawing;
The sun had begun its descent,
And another day lost,
Another lover laments.

These ports that brought white storms and black
plagues,
The seas behest was the shores impetus.
Far away, she wondered,
Was he carrion or was he well?
The hand that bid adieu,
Had it turned bitter?

In time, all will fade,
Memories become bad dreams,
Memoirs become fiction,
The tale of a love lost at sea: becomes cliché,
The port bustles and business awaits.

-Vin

Flower

She was drenched from yesterday's drizzle
The droplets kissing her silky petals,
Basking in the glory of the sleepy sun.
She was dressed in her finest white
Ready to shame the fairest bride.
And soon she be drowning in suitors,
Busy bees and bright butterflies.
And so she bloomed,
An intoxicating scent set free.
A beauty amongst bitter brutes.

-Vin

Upon my Death

The day has dawned but I haven't;
I'm to be buried deep in her bowels.

But fell not wood for my casket nor tears for my
parting;
Send me away with an unknown poet's verse,
To honor the muse that once was.
Send me away with a wilted rose,
For the courage to love was never mine.
Send me away with a pen so bare,
To bade farewell to the words never penned.
Send me away one last time.

Let me rest in the endless blue,
Amidst life and forever adrift;
No tombstones or annual flowers,
Just a memory to fade with time.

-Vin

Meadow

A journey through the land of my fathers,
On a railroad sanctioned by colonial masters.
I was left with pensive thoughts and perilous
dreams,
When a glint of green danced on groggy eyes.
A meadow stretched on till trees played walls,
Adorned with cotton clouds and an ocean blue
shawl.
Through tinted windows I saw the pastures
thrive,
For a moment there I fancied a simpler life.

The train gave no heed to my viridescent
reflection,
Rattling along to my ticketed destination.

-Vin

Intoxicating Passion

A little tingling as my lips brushed yours,
Our hearts beating to our carnal cravings;
Beads of sweat glistening on our backs,
As the dance of desire achieves a raucous
rhythm.

The melodies were crooned,
The medleys were played;
Our bodies became bare,
Our souls became one.

The warmth of Pleasure engulfs our being,
Whilst the air bristled with a fiery fervor.
A passion of perils at the zenith of indulgence,
The dance had reached its dizzying crescendo.

The dancers collapsed
Drenched in perspiration
and drunk in pleasure;
They were taken by the silent night.

-Vin

Amorous Addiction

The smoke that spews from the burning end,
That's all he was to her;
The means to an end,
An afterthought to wile away the hours.
He felt her warm breath on his skin,
Mistook it as love's gentle tingling;
But it was his lungs that burnt black,
She took his breath away and his dying breath.

She made him pledge obsequence,
He served her well longing for the lost glow.
She was his undoing,
An addiction he could never shake.

-Vin

An Unlikely Companion

A sullied sleep and a severed dream,
The chill of a morning yet to rise
Sent a shiver through my bones.
My day was to begin two hours yonder,
Head still reeling from earlier ephialtes.

I sought peace on my window sill,
An inner soliloquy gathering momentum;
And at this moment, I found an unlikely
companion.
A moth whose manner matched mine.
He humored my scruples with no air of
judgment,
Let my tirade take its course.
Glimmers of gold started to appear,
It was time to bid him goodbye.

Sleep abandoned me & a moth kept me
company,
It sure was an unusual morning.

-Vin

Ruby

The precious red,
The perilous red,
The passionate red.

At a simpler time your beauty had me swooning;
But when you were at my fingertips,
You were more than the glamorous red.
In your edges, I saw my blemishes;
Your contours revealed my calloused palms.

Many a night I've dreamt of your scarlet
splendor,
Now I long for the nights that passed.

The precious red,
The perilous red,
The passionate red.

You were a curse I never deserved.

-Vin

The Web

The itsy bitsy spider went about its business,
Spewing symmetry with infallible finesse.
The silky threads seemed beautiful and bare,
They be a trap that little fleas need beware.

Elegant and dangerous:
The artist and the art.
The spider weaves perfection
not for applause neither attention;
The nuance was bred for a more trivial cause:
Necessity birthed an 8-legged maestro.

-Vin

Fading Memory

Sometimes it's a smell,
Oftentimes it's a passing thought.
Sending cracks along the walls once built,
Giving in to the whims of turbulent waters.

But that once awakened a sleeping monster,
Now just annoys a wandering stray.

Little by little,
Let Time do his magic.

Allow the memories to fade,
but he'll never let them die.

-Vin

Another Sunset

It was his last,
Tomorrow is no more to cherish,
He's been given hours closing in on minutes;
There were no flurry of images,
Nor was a longing for another dawn.
However,
He saw a silhouette in that sunset.
A silhouette in her prime.

There were many before
And there will be many more.

Another sun had set and so did the simpleton...

-Vin

Sunflower

She that blooms at the break of dawn,
With golden petals to match the amber morn.
She sways and swivels to Apollo's whims,
A beauty that could shame the fabled nymphs.

When the mind be ambushed by the perils of
men,
Picture the Sunflower in a glory so innocent;
To rise with the sun and rest after his adieu,
An image to remember for the next Monday
blue.

-Vin

The Desert's Allure

The Desert beckons to the fair maiden,
A sojourn worth a fortnight;
Like the sand that succumbs to the wind's
whims,
Her heart was swept away by the golden grain.
She fancied a home in the little oasis,
With lively lambs and philosophical camels to
keep her company;
The chilly nights her trusted confidante.

But she was an interloper in this barren beauty;
The song of the desert eluded her,
His secrets were hidden from her gaze.

Many years later in that soulless metropolis,
Her dreams fly her back to that Arabian
Paradise.

-Vin

Fallen Angel

Given wings and gifted sins,
He was what was made of him;
Punished to reign over the wretched,
He echoes the wrath of quenched rebellion.

Likened to beasts and made to wear evil's livery,
He be blamed for man's misdemeanors;
Rivers of blood & rivulets of tears,
He is beyond salvation.
Hear! Hear! The murky melodies;
The Fallen yearns to be felled.

-Vin

The City

Neon jewels adorned the concrete 'scrapers,
Twinkling to the envy of the stars;
Millions walked on her cobbled streets,
All fighting to survive rush hour fleets.

The City is more than her dazzle and noise.
She rises before the sun,
Breathes with the moon and holds her poise;
She answers to many but begets none.

The City is man's trepid tapestry,
Woven to perfection but brittle to the blaze...

-Vin

The Last Light

Careful but coy,
She was the last of us.
But her gold was loosing it's shine,
Her breath sputtering away;
She was soon to be one with the dark.

It was then she remembered a promise,
A promise made under a sanguine sun:
"We'll be better but never bitter,
We'll love but never leave,
We'll suffer but never sacrifice"

The promise died with her
And hope followed her into the black beyond.

-Vin

Mon Chère Rose

At a time when peace reigned undisputed
And prosperity flowed freer than wine,
A boy longed for adventure in lands far away and
difficult for the tongue.
But to hope is a hapless future
And he fell head first into that ravine.

He toiled for hours and trembled at alms,
The pride of youth faded to faint echoes.
But there appeared sprinkles of joy,
Salt to his mortal wounds.
He kept neither wife nor friends to mourn,
For he feared loss and the flames of old.

The time came for a will to be written
But what do fallen men own?
He bequeathed his misery and bested his breath.
Morning came.....
The letter at his dangling foot read, 'Mon Chère
Rose'

-Vin

Lady of The Night

Yuletide melodies and a whiff of cold air,
ill tidings and a bad hand was dealt,
He found promise in the sun to rise.
A lady of the night took pity on his plight,
"Here", she said.
"A shoulder to cry and warmth for the night".
But the price was not right for a man so
wretched,
The livery of misery reeked of cheap cigarettes.

She moved on to more promising mites,
He held on to her tawdry scent.
Tomorrow he returned to match the price,
Would that suffice to pay for his vice?

-Vin

A Graduate's Soliloquy

Carefree, careless and a caress of joy;
Bygone days as Dionysus's envoy.
The chitter, the chatter and the endless prattle,
Can't help but miss a student's mantle.

All good things must come to an end,
Time to say goodbyes and make amends.
The world awaits and freedom abates,
Onwards we march, trepidant yet tall!

-Vin

Selene

As the twilight red fades to a Stygian light,
She is called by the creatures of the night.
Enamoring a few and escorting others,
She was close but always a bit farther.

The night grows weary as her chariot whittles by,
A silent paean sung across the sky.

Her countenance fades with the nights to come,
Beloved Selene, In Perpetuum et Unum Diem!

-Vin

The Balance

Darkness cradles the light,
Akin to love and endorsed by hate,
Cradle life with kisses in spite;
The hunters circle the worshipping prey.

Benign thy heart, barren thy soul,
The preachers come bearing iatric venom;
Brute and mellow hand in hand,
Bestowing hell on heavenly canvas.

The balance that blunders but never wrought
asunder,
Bask in the glory of its brazen silhouette.

-Vin

Reluctant Recluse

Monsoon rains and mild melodramas,
It's a melody I've hummed but never sung.
Time's aplenty,
The silence punctuated by coughing frogs;
No offer to parley and none for peace.

The humdrum's amiss,
The daily grind, a distant memory.
Among the many deprived pleasures,
Seclusion singes the most sanguine of souls.

Unbeknownst or unbecoming,
The facade is no more than mere fragments.

-Vin

Unholy Sacrifice

He would be remiss to not reminisce,
Middle-aged is the title or for euphemism's sake
He was entering the youth of old-age.
Success was writ across his walls,
But age played spoilsport with irony's magic
dust:
He has lived too long to hold his Victories dear.

Aged far beyond the thrill of youth,
The trophies continued to collect dust.

Bygone days of freedom and frivolity,
A lifetime ago in the fringes of his mind,
Akin to a waking dream that lingered too long.
The Man of focus who sought to please &
appease his illustrious patronage.

With borrowed ambition and a hand-me-down
dream,
He dug his space,
One step behind the crème de la crème.

The petulant chords reverberate across empty
halls,
Senility shaken & serenity sunk in sordid
servitude.
A mad man roamed these halls,
With a madness so lucid,
Psychedelic trances were shamed and shunned.

The sacrifice that yields disproportionate
dividends;
Time, temptation & other tempests worn thin as
the corpse's veil.
His Will and Testament was all that remained of
this Sacred life...

-Vin

Faith in a Butterfly

Wings that dance to the sun's beat,
Your dainty hues serve as my eyes' retreat.
Of the many woodland nymphs & crafty fauns,
The myth of your luster excites me more.

When the horizon darkens and the sun's gone
long,
A fleeting memory about a fluttering soul
Reignites hope in this stranded poeticule.

- Vin

Paris

The scent of freshly baked bread wafting through
the halls,
With the Parisian sun budding over the city of
love.
A dream worth a smile and a tired chuckle.

To bask in the beauty and stroll through those
rues,
Sipping coffee and waiting for dusk,
To feel the beat of the city of lights,
Is a wish worth the longing.

Dine in sight of La Tour Eiffel
With glistening white wine for company.
A walk along the Seine while the air dances to a
Busker's flute.
It sure is a prize worth fighting for!

A morning of culture and a night of romance,
Oh dear! It's the ultimate trance.

- Vin

Among Us

The sound of rustling leaves drowned the noise
of the storm.
The tempest will soon drown the forest.
The nymphs' parley bore no fruit, the mighty oak
resigned to his fate.
It is upon us, among the woodland creatures
both high and low.
The night approaches and the cold stings worse
than the nettle.
Nobody to fight, nowhere to flee.
Bury your brethren and brave the winters, it is
among us.

-Vin

A Moment More

You were mine & I was yours,
The passion tingled & the love flowed
Like the mystical rivers of old.
But like all good things,
We caved to the whims of the world.

There followed moment of revelry,
Moments of sadness,
Moments of peace,
Moments of peril.

Life was sour but savory,
The seasons came and so did the greys,
Self-reflection set into my ways.
Then came the thought I've trained to ignore...

A Moment More in your embrace,
A Moment More to kiss you anew.

Another new year's eve,
A bottle of wine but just the lone glass,
To muddle the senses and lull the mind.
The memories do fade but the moments,
The moments remain resolute!

-Vin

Beneath the Trees

Through the shade of darkness,
A humid night approaches.
An owl hoots to heed its prey,
The deluge due south is on its way.

The night gets longer
as the lone light gets bolder.
The times have changed
though the troubles do remain.

Beneath the trees on a bitter road,
His peace for the pennies traded.

-Vin

To the Unknown

Two steps at a time,
Towards the great mystery;
One step back,
Cuz of fate's hystory.
The eyes don't see the great beyond,
The heart pounds for what's ahead.

In light of lessons learnt,
In search of better fortunes.
To the unknown when the fog clears;
Two steps at a time, One step back.

-Vin

Happy Place

The sun was anew & the sky was blue,
The river lapped on my muddy shoes.
When the hues of dawn dwindled on,
I left for home a Content Man.

Dark days now, dreary ones ahead;
A dainty day deigns only in dreams.
In my horrors & in my errors,
My mind still fades to that Happy Place.

-Vin

Legacy

The winds will come,
They will come for me
To erase my footsteps from the sand;
The darkness too, for my sight.

In that void a memory strikes:
A forlorn shell abandoned ashore.
She held the sea in her curves,
Her shell smoothened by caressing waves.
A trinket of nascent whims held my remnants...

It's since been long,
My name is long forgotten.

A delicate legacy washes ashore,
She who held the sea in her curves.

-Vin

The City

Felt old in his bones,
The city had done its time;
By his lonesome at the break of dawn,
He walked through paths not his own.
The end was near & the edge was nigh,
His chest heaved its hundredth sigh.

Come daybreak to dash the damned fog,
His sight cleared but not his ailing lungs.

Overmorrow or for all eternity,
The city was never his...

-Vin

Last Tulip

On a summer lovelorn,
Dreaming of a field of tulips,
Far in the meadows due South,
Where the winter left nothing of worth

It was the great red rage,
The world beholden in a bitter cage.
Morsels continued to rain,
Grief percolated through all the pain.

War was waged, the veterans long gone;
The Last Tulip withered away thay morn.

-Vin

Land of Letters

Far beyond borders,
Between wooden shelves with worn nails,
Lies the mysteries of love and lore;
Where fairies bring you luck,
Where fantasy leaves you awestruck.

When life loses its listless charm,
Let the Land of Letters claim you for its own...

-Vin

'morrow

75

The Gift of new beginnings,
The Gulf of past sorrows;
Sail across them, Good Soldier!
This be your chance to cleanse the blood of
yesteryear ...

Believe what can't be forgotten;
Bequeath what can't be bested.
As in love, so be in life -
The reward is today, never tomorrow ...

The Gulf of past sorrows,
The Gift of new beginnings.

-Vin

On the Other Side

Intoxicated by her scent,
Incarcerated by the distance;
She was a stone's throw away,
He stood entrenched in a sea of sand:
The moment reeked of perceptive perfection.

So be it and so it should be,
The tale of tomorrow dies tonight.
A hand in friendship, abother in farewell;
Basking in the snow of that festive night,
He found himself cornered on the other side.

-Vin

Marooned

He awoke to the gentle embrace of the tides,
A Man who embodied the ol' "woe betide".
Broken, beaten, battered and bruised,
The promised darkness was a touch too tardy.

As he waited for his due reprieve,
The scent of the sea stirred memories of home.
Scant furniture and muddled memoirs,
There wasn't much too leave behind.

And as the peace claimed his final breath;
The Man's death was much akin to the life he led
...

-Vin

Frost

Icicles as far as the eye can see,
A daydream draped in delightful glee;
Blessed by the white of morn,
Saddled in a snow sensuously borne.

Like ghosts from bygone bards,
The frost frolicked on timbered yards;
Bejeweled by the nagging northern chills,
A sight to rival faraway wonderlands.

Hugged by the cold & held in wintertide,
The dawn bore witness to beauty personified.

-Vin

Unsolved Puzzle

79

On a nightly haze when the mind was dazed,
They traversed a troubling maze.
The eyes were glazed, their will unfazed,
Onwards they went at an uneasy pace.

The shadows grew long,
The question remained:
"Is it right to be in the wrong?"
To err was fate ordained.

The pieces were lost, the peace muzzled,
And so You remained an unsolved puzzle...

-Vin

Hunt for Home

On the move without a treasure trove,
The Boy that left the shaded grove
came to face what fate behooved.
Wilted roses & weathered steps,
The house was beat beyond reprieve.

And so begins the search...

He looked far and farther still,
In the darkest towns & brightest hills,
With calloused feet and a callow heart,
The pursuit of home stifled his spirit.

On the beaten path he made his home,
Far from fealty and farther from hope;
The quest invoked the heartless victor:
Irony!
(He who hunted for home, died a vagabond...)

-Vin

Locked Away

Deep in the crevices of the damned heart,
Pierced by the dame & pillaged by the same,
A sputtering flame heaves its final sigh;
And down it goes into the dark depths of
winterfell.

In the ashes a promise festers;
Unsaid, Unwritten, Unclaimed:
"To fell by the sword, we will;
To fell by the heart, we won't"

And so begins the night
When promises were ripped with brazen might;
Far was the glory of the final flight,
The warrior crumbled to the weakened heart's
plight.

Broken was the will of unbreakable men,
The promise of old fell prey to pain;
Lock away the beating betrayer 'nd bury deep
the key,
That be the only way to break the shackles free.

Too early yet too late to make haste;
The taste of you titters in the hands of fate.

-Vin

Image of the Father

And so the river awakens to the gold of dawn,
Amber be the waters, admiring the glory of
morn.
For this day he was born,
Bearing the strength of those long gone.

As the rivers reflect the might of the sun,
He basks in the strength of those before him.
To honor the name and the blood in his veins,
That familial fealty be his divine duty.

And so strives the son in the battles to follow,
Will he ever be worthy of his father's name?

-Vin

Golden Battle

The foliage of fall & the feverish fallen,
Tinged a glorious golden by the gong of
sundown,
The dusk lingers on to deny the dark,
A losing battle lurks beyond the hallowed mark:
Victory is in sight for the nefarious night.

Bleeding pink on the flanks of fall,
The fallen bid goodbye as they near Valhalla's
hall.
Fleeing forward to the fear of overmorrow,
The golden warriors hold strong to their soulless
sorrows:
Defeat is imminent for the dying dusk.

Her scent lingered on and so did the memories
of her;
Buried by wintertide, beneath the fallens' grave.

- Vin

When the Light Fades

To all before and for those to come,
A melody in green grasps the night.
Dance of disdain and dazzling desperation,
The last of fall lusts for winter's lullaby.
Curtains drop at the urban cliff,
The show must end before the morning grief.

Here comes tomorrow, gloriously gold;
Burying the green and its midnight sheen.

Locked deep within that lackluster mind,
A memory persists with divine perseverance;
Where city lights were put to shame
By the frolicking of the green due north.

When the light fades and so does the mind,
That moment will never be left behind...

- Vin

Snow Squall

85

So strings the busker
a melody far warmer;
The tempest rages
with temperament not tender.
So succumbs the town to the Yuletide lull.

Once more, the sorrows of yesteryear,
soon to be sullied by holiday Joy...

-Vin

Beyond

The lore of heavens lies atop,
Where snow seduces while the cloud eludes.
Myth, magic and mirthless winds,
The motley melts to the morose

To gaze beyond the rocks of old,
Beyond the lore of men and more,
To call and recall the voices gone,
The mortal cedes to the mystic beyond.

-Vin

* 9 7 8 9 3 6 0 9 4 3 3 1 8 *